JANE GOODALL
IN CONVERSATION

Shaping a Better Future for Our Planet

Edited by John Chryssavgis

Brookline, Massachusetts

In collaboration with Akritas Publications, Athens, Greece.

Published by
Holy Cross Orthodox Press
50 Goddard Avenue
Brookline, MA 02445

ISBN: 978-1-960613-13-4 print
978-1-960613-16-5 epub

Photos: Kelly Cunha, Deborah J. Levine

Publishers Cataloging-in-Publication
(Provided by Cassidy Cataloguing Services, Inc.)
Names: Chryssavgis, John, editor. | Holy Cross Greek Orthodox School of Theology. Huffington Ecumenical Institute, sponsoring body.
Title: Jane Goodall in conversation : shaping a better future for our planet / edited by John Chryssavgis.
Description: Brookline, Massachusetts : Holy Cross Orthodox Press, [2026] | Sponsored by the Huffington Ecumenical Institute at Hellenic College Holy Cross School of Theology.-- Introduction.
Identifiers: ISBN: 9781960613134 (print) | 9781960613165 (epub)
Subjects: LCSH: Goodall, Jane, 1934-2025--Political and social views. | Sustainability. | Environmentalism. | Environmental responsibility. | Environmental protection. | Human ecology. | Social ethics.
Classification: LCC: HC79.E5 J36 2026 | DDC: 363.7--dc23

CONTENTS

ECUMENISM SHAPING A BETTER FUTURE FOR OUR PLANET:

A DISCUSSION BETWEEN JANE GOODALL & JOHN CHRYSSAVGIS

Dr. Jane Goodall -renowned primatologist, anthropologist, and recognized environmentalist will share her thoughts on the power of ecumenical encounters and dialogue in shaping a better future for our planet. The talk inaugurates HEI's Ecumenical Conversations Series and will take place on Wednesday, September 27 at 11:30 AM at the Maliotis Cultural Center of Hellenic College Holy Cross, 50 Goddard Avenue, Brookline, MA 02445.

The visit is a unique opportunity for and open to students of the Hellenic College and Holy Cross Greek Orthodox School of Theology, the Boston Theological Inter-religious Consortium, and the wider local community interested in learning first-hand about the extraordinary experiences and insights of Dr. Goodall on a mission to empower and educate youth in making the world a better place through her internationally acclaimed Roots & Shoots program.
Dr. Goodall will hold a -free and open to the public- conversation with Fr. John Chryssavgis, Executive Director of the newly-established Huffington Ecumenical Institute at Hellenic College Holy Cross.

INTRODUCTION

This publication marks the inception of a series of books produced by the Huffington Ecumenical Institute at Hellenic College Holy Cross School of Theology for the purpose of highlighting some of the contributions from the institute's extensive programming. It also launches a collaboration with Akritas Books in Greece that will jointly publish select manuscripts of common interest.

Endowed by the Honorable Michael Huffington in 2022 and established at Holy Cross School of Theology in 2023, the institute aims to address contemporary issues and social challenges facing our century and the world through ecumenical dialogue and theological scholarship. Accordingly, the institute's objective is to facilitate and advance conversation and cooperation—particularly around theological and ethical, as well as pastoral and practical questions—by exploring and expressing the fundamental ethos of the Orthodox Church in open encounter and honest engagement with other confessions and religions, along with other academic institutions and scientific disciplines. This is how we, at the Huffington Ecumenical Institute, perceive the heart and pulse of ecumenical relations.

As a result, on a yearly basis, we host many events, programs, courses, and conferences, welcoming church leaders and distinguished scholars, while involving speakers and students, who engage the campus community and wider society on diverse theological and topical questions. This series of books will highlight some of the inspirational and influential moments in the varied agenda of our institute.

I am grateful in advance for the collaboration of Akritas Books and the diligence of my colleagues on the Editorial Committee: Elena Kontogli, Assistant Executive Director (HEI); Marilyn Rouvelas, Senior Editorial Advisor; and Ben Malian (MTS, cand.) who prepared the interview transcript.

The first volume in the series emerged from an interview hosted by the Institute at the Maliotis Cultural Center of Hellenic College Holy Cross School of Theology with Dr. Jane Goodall (Jane Goodall Institute) in September 2023.

The conversation focuses on the plight of the natural environment from Dr. Goodall's experience in Gombe. The discussion with Jane, whom I had invited to the first Halki Summit of the Ecumenical Patriarchate in 2012, was actually the inaugural event of the Huffington Ecumenical Institute.

John Chryssavgis

INTRODUCTION TO THE GREEK EDITION

This edition signals the beginning of a new collaboration between Akritas Publications in Athens and the Huffington Ecumenical Institute at Hellenic College Holy Cross School of Theology. It is our hope that this partnership will raise awareness among Greek readers about personalities and subjects that cannot leave any of us indifferent. The emblematic presence and influential work of Jane Goodall, as illuminated in her vibrant dialogue with Fr. John Chryssavgis, make this the ideal inaugural volume in a series that we trust will continue with the same enthusiasm and inspiration that it promises to all of us—publishers and readers alike. Our warmest thanks go to Fr. John Chryssavgis and his team, as well as to Bishop Anthony of Synada, for this beautiful initial collaboration. Without their steadfast presence, none of this would have been possible.

Maria D. Kokkinou

BIOGRAPHICAL NOTE

Dr. Jane Goodall—Dame Commander of the British Empire, Founder of the Jane Goodall Institute, and United Nations Messenger of Peace—was born on April 3, 1934, in London, England. At the young age of twenty-six, she followed her passion for animals and Africa to Gombe, Tanzania, where she began her landmark study of chimpanzees in the wild, immersing herself in their habitat as a neighbor rather than a distant observer. Her discovery in 1960 that chimpanzees make and use tools rocked the scientific world and redefined the relationship between humans and animals.

In 1977, she established the Jane Goodall Institute (JGI) to advance her work around the world and for generations to come. JGI continues the field research at Gombe and builds on Dr. Goodall's innovative approach to conservation, which recognizes the central role that local communities play in the protection of animals and the environment. In 1991, she founded “Roots & Shoots,” a global program that empowers young people in over seventy-five countries and since its inception has had a positive impact on members around the world. It has greatly impacted young people in over one hundred countries to act as the informed conservation leaders that the world so urgently needs.

Dr. Goodall traveled throughout the world, speaking about the threats to the natural world—such as climate change and loss of biodiversity, the need to address the ever-growing environmental crisis, and the reasons to hope that it is not too late to reverse the harm we have caused. In her books and speeches, she emphasized the interconnectedness of all living things and the collective power of individual action.

On September 24, 2025, Dr. Goodall attended the ceremony at the Lincoln Center in New York City, where His All-Holiness Ecumenical Patriarch Bartholomew was awarded the Templeton Prize. She died on October 1, 2025.

Original video link:

https://www.youtube.com/watch?v=Onp9lT_5JHA&t=1s

The following interview has been edited and expanded in collaboration with Jane Goodall. This interview is based on a conversation between Dr. Jane Goodall and Fr. John Chryssavgis. The event was hosted by the Huffington Ecumenical Institute at Holy Cross Greek Orthodox School of Theology on September 27, 2023, at the Maliotis Cultural Center in Brookline, Massachusetts. I am grateful to Jane for accepting to be our inaugural speaker at the institute.

INTERVIEW

Fr. John Chryssavgis (JC): Jane, I'd like to welcome you to the Huffington Ecumenical Institute at Hellenic College-Holy Cross Greek Orthodox School of Theology. I have just returned from a conference in Budapest, where I accompanied His All-Holiness Ecumenical Patriarch Bartholomew, who sends his warmest greetings. He was delighted that you would be on our campus, the flagship seminary of the Greek Orthodox Archdiocese in this country. It's truly wonderful to have you here.

It is literally just three weeks since I assumed responsibilities as the inaugural executive director of this new Ecumenical Institute sponsored and endowed by the Honorable Michael Huffington. And you, are in fact, our very first official visitor and speaker. I could never have asked for something bigger or better. Because your unique personality and your global work summarize the mission of the institute as I envisage it—namely, discerning and determining ways in which people of all denominations and persuasions, as well as of all disciplines and good will, can work together to respect and protect the precious gift of God's creation, both the planet and its people.

Dr. Jane Goodall (JG): So do you also have a brand-new visitor's book for me to sign?!

JC: We haven't even had time to secure a guest book. But we will make sure you sign something that we can frame. Your email accepting to come here, at the tail end of a busy schedule in Boston, is in itself sufficient reason to frame!

Let me begin by saying that I don't think it is by accident you are at a seminary. I know you do not in principle promote your work as religious, although you have spent time among people in church congregations and faith communities. Indeed, you have visited Istanbul and served as keynote speaker at an environmental summit organized by the Ecumenical Patriarchate. But you also have talked about your work in religious terms. You have certainly talked to me about your work as being nothing less than a *mission*. You have mentioned that you feel you have a mission to accomplish, that you have been placed here on this earth for a reason, and that you can hardly find enough time to fulfil this work adequately. That's why you travel across the whole world. I cannot even recount the number and names of the countries you have been to in the last two weeks. You've been throughout the United States; and during this visit to Massachusetts, in the space of two days, you have spoken to adults and children at the Science Museum of Boston, to a public audience at the Chevalier Theater in Medford, and to a school in Plymouth. So your focus—*your vision*—is undeniably ecumenical! This is precisely why I thought it would fit very comfortably into the vision of our Ecumenical Institute.

Tell us a little bit about the religious or Christian roots of your own family. And tell us how you see your vision.

JG: Well, it all started with my Welsh grandfather. Sadly, I never met him; he died of cancer before I was born. He was a Congregational minister and towards the end of his life he was highly respected, and appointed to the Congregation church in Bournemouth, known as the 'Cathedral of the Congregational Church.' I am sad that I never actually got to know him.

Jane Goodall at the Huffington Ecumenical Institute at HCHC (2023)

When I was young, we didn't go to church every Sunday. We were not what you would call a particularly "religious" family. But we were undoubtedly a Christian family. My grandmother—Danny, as she was known (because when I was little I could not say 'Gr')—had what she called a "Bible Box." It had little drawers with texts from the Bible in it that you could pull out. But when I looked at them, they were all sort of bland. They were all, you know, the sort of nice soothing ones you read in scripture. So as a Christmas present for Danny—I think I was fourteen at the time—I read the Bible every night; and I read through every single chapter, carefully writing down the verses that made me think that we need to be awakened and attentive, we need to obey the commandments. They were written on tiny strips of paper rolled up tightly. These were placed inside six little matchboxes glued together, which I still have. Sometimes, when I am about to set off on yet another tour and feel so tired, I grumble to my sister that I really don't want to go, she will reach for the matchboxes and tell me to choose a text. And *three times* I've picked out—can you guess what text? The one that says: "He who has once set his hand to the plough and turneth back is not fit for the Kingdom of Heaven" (Luke 9.62). And so Judy says to me: "Off you go, stop grousing!" It's pretty amazing because each match box holds about thirty texts, and we always put them back in a different order.

When I was fifteen, I fell in love—quite platonically, I hasten to add—with the Welsh parson Trevor Davis who was appointed to the church. He preached amazing sermons. And it was because of him that Jesus became real to me. And then I attended regularly, going to every service possible just so I could listen to Trevor talk with that beautiful Welsh lilt. But when I left school and got a job in London, I was no longer going to church and gradually religion became a less important part of my life. Some years later, after I had started my work studying the chimpanzees, I was invited to a conference in Paris. I had always wanted to go to Notre Dame Cathedral—so now was my chance. I was going through a rather difficult time in my life. I went quite early in the morning as the sun was just coming through the great rose window. Apparently, there was a wedding going on somewhere; and as I was gazing, entranced, at that glorious window, quite suddenly the organ came to life, and Bach's

Jane Goodall on meeting His All-Holiness Ecumenical Patriarch Bartholomew for the first time at Halki Summit I (2012)

Toccata in D minor filled the cathedral. And suddenly I was thinking about how it was that I was standing there, at that moment in time. I thought of all the couplings, all the individuals who gave birth to children—children who owed their lives to the meeting of their parents. And the children in turn found partners and themselves produced children. And I thought of all the different clergy who had preached in the cathedral, the architect who built it. Was it all chance, I asked myself, that led to my family, to me? Could it be chance that ended up in this one moment? I felt, at that moment, that it wasn't. And if it wasn't chance, then it was non-chance. It was God. I do believe in free will, that you are free to make choices in which direction you will take. But I also believe there is a path laid out, and it is up to you whether you follow it or not.

JC: You once also told me that you are doing the best you can do here on this planet. And you wondered whether that would be enough time and enough fruitful achievement to allow you into the Kingdom or anywhere else. I have to admit, I would like to be wherever you go. If you go to the Kingdom, I'm coming with you. If you go elsewhere, I'm going there, too!

JG: Well, I'm only going if there are dogs there as well!

JC: There are religious overtones to the work you are doing—the work of our Patriarch certainly has religious dimensions. His environmental work is not merely social or political. It is deeply theological and spiritual. Religion clearly impacts this kind of work, but religion is also in turn impacted by it and should be impacted by it. It's a two-way relationship. I am always wary when religion claims to have the answers to everything. I think religion has a lot to learn, for example, from anthropology and science. At the same time, there is a sense in which your work transcends religion. That is again what I would describe as the ecumenical dimension. Your work appeals to so many different peoples, so many different religions, so many different cultures. That is abundantly clear just by looking at a map of where you have been over the years. How do you perceive your work as a sort of common objective for all peoples and all religions?

JG: I love the fact that, in every major religion, there is the same golden rule: "Do unto others as you would have them do unto you"

Jane Goodall with His All-Holiness Ecumenical Patriarch Bartholomew at the Templeton Prize Ceremony (2025)

(Matthew 7.12). And if we include animals and the environment in with the "others"—what a beautiful world this would be! In the Commandments, we read: "Thou shalt not kill" (Exodus 20.13). Yet we are not obeying it. And by the way, "Thou shalt not kill" should include animals, too. Not just human animals.

When I am out in the forest, I feel this strong spiritual connection with a great Spiritual Power. I was sitting in the forest one day and was contemplating this Spiritual Power. Looking at a little insect on a tree, a flower pushing through the damp soil and a bird singing overhead, I thought: "If we have what we call a soul, then it is surely a spark of the divine in us. If so, then these other creatures and plants also have a spark of the divine in them; then surely they too have souls. We are all one living connected life force." It was the most amazing feeling of being a part of nature that I can only experience when I am alone. Because when I am alone, the fact that I am human is not even part of the equation. I am there, just there—a part of this community of spiritual beings.

JC: It's interesting that you speak of connections: connections with nature and connections with God. Can you say something more about this?

JG: For me, the more I learn about the wonder of the natural world, the more science reveals about the incredible diversity of plants and animal, the more I feel convinced that, as more scientists believe, there is an intelligence behind the design of the universe. In the forest I felt a close connection with the Great Spiritual Being—known by different names by different religions. It was my mother who told me that all must refer to the same Supreme Being. Growing up in the Christian religion I would call this spiritual being God or Christ. But had I grown up a different religion, I would call this Being: Allah or Jehovah, Krishna or Shiva, Creator or Buddha. And there are many other names for the Creator in religions around the world.

It was my wise mother who believed there could be only one God, despite all the names people gave to the deity they worshiped. How wonderful it would be if the religions of the world would get together and help people understand that we need to stop harming Planet Earth, created by the One God, and start healing the wounds we have created—before it is too late. I strongly believe that there is a window of time after which, if we carry on with business as usual, the heat will make it impossible for life, as we know it, to survive. Humans are not exempt from extinction.

JC: In many ways, this interconnectedness is precisely what religion should be all about. Learning and affirming that we are intimately and inseparably connected with one another, with nature, and with God; isn't that what prayer is all about?

JG: I have talked to you about the wonderful life I had when I was out in the forest. The more I was immersed in this forest world for hours each day with the chimpanzees or sometimes entirely by myself, I got a stronger and stronger feeling about connection to this great spiritual power I call God. That presence was all around me. And I got this feeling that if I accidentally crushed a plant, trod on an insect or harmed nature in any way I would be harming God. And once you feel that this spiritual interconnectedness with the natural world is connected to God, you start thinking in a different way.

JC: You're almost describing your relationship with David Greybeard now, aren't you?

Jane Goodall with Mr. H. at Halki Summit I (2012)

JG: You want me to speak about David Greybeard, don't you?

JC: That's a good place to start.

JG: As you know, a lot of my life was initially devoted to learning about our closest living relative, the chimpanzee. Now my job is to give animals a voice in gatherings such as this around the world so that they may be better understood.

David Greybeard was the first chimpanzee to lose his fear of me. For four whole months the others all vanished into the forest whenever they saw me. I only had money for six months for my research. I had not even been to university; we could not afford it. So it had been very difficult for my mentor, Louis Leakey,[1] to raise even the money for six months. People were slightly shocked that a young girl from England, who had no degree, was being sent off into a forest to tackle what nobody else had done—to

[1] Louis Leakey (1903–1972) was a Kenyan-British palaeoanthropologist and archaeologist whose work was important in demonstrating that humans evolved in Africa, particularly through discoveries made at Olduvai Gorge with his wife, fellow palaeoanthropologist Mary Leakey.

learn about chimpanzees in the wild. Gombe was in what was then Tanganyika (now Tanzania), which was a British protectorate, and the British authorities initially refused permission. They did not want responsibility for that young girl. Leakey finally persuaded them, but was told that I could not go alone, and it was my wonderful mother who volunteered to come with me. So that is how the long-term study of the Gombe chimpanzees (now in its sixty-sixth year) began with my mother and me, a second-hand army tent, a minimum of equipment and food and a Tanzanian cook, Dominic. We were told we had to have a cook. Moreover, I had absolutely no guidelines as to how I should go about the study.

JC: You've often said that your mother played a critical role in nurturing your love for nature and animals.

JG: Yes, indeed. How amazingly lucky I was (if it was luck?) to have an amazing and supportive mother. I credit her for enabling me to become who I am today. I was born with a love of all animals, and mum supported that love. I spent all the time I could out in nature. I had a special tree , Beech, in the garden, and I would climb up to spend hours there just feeling close to the birds and the sky. When I was growing up there was no television. I learned from being in nature and from books. I loved books. We had little money, but I would save my few pennies of pocket money to buy books (my sister saved hers for sweets!). I discovered a funny little secondhand book shop and spent hours there every Saturday. When I was ten years old, I found a small edition of *Tarzan of the Apes* and had just enough money to buy it. I fell in love with Tarzan; I was really jealous that he married the *wrong* Jane. It was that book which gave me the desire to go to Africa, to live with wild animals and write books about them. Everybody laughed at me. Back then World War II was still raging. Africa was known as "the dark continent;" how could I, as a girl, do something like that? Boys were the ones that received the adventurous chances in life. "Jane, dream about something you can achieve," I was told. But not by my mother; she would say: "If you really want something, and you work hard and you never give up, you will find a way."

JC: That is such formative advice at that tender age. Do you recall any specific moments or memories when this advice played out during your childhood?

JG: One of my favorite memories is when she once took me to stay on a farm in the countryside. We lived in London at the time and there were not many animals in the neighborhood, just pigeons and sparrows. It was a proper farm where animals grazed in the fields. I was just four years old, and my task was to collect the hens' eggs. There were about six or seven little hen houses where they slept at night to keep them safe from foxes, and it was where the hens laid their eggs in the straw of nest boxes. I had to lift the lid of these and, if there were any eggs, pop them into my basket. Apparently, I began to ask everybody, "Where is the hole big enough for an egg to come out?" I couldn't see a hole like that, and nobody gave me a proper answer.

I vividly remember seeing a hen, she was brown, heading into one of the hen houses. It was about 2:00 pm and I must have thought: "Oh, she's going to lay an egg!" So I crawled inside the henhouse after her. That was a big mistake. She squawked and flapped out in fear. My little brain must have thought: "Well, no hens will lay here, they will think there is

Jane Goodall with Fr. John Chryssavgis at Halki Summit I (2012)

something dangerous inside." But now I was on the path of discovery, and I would find the answer to my question myself. So I climbed into an empty henhouse and just waited and waited and waited. Finally, I watched as a hen came in, scratched the straw into a sort of nest, and laid an egg! I'm not sure who was more pleased, the hen or me.

By this time, of course, my mother was at the point of calling the police. I had disappeared for four hours! Imagine a little girl of four gone for four hours! So many mothers would have grabbed that child and chided them: "How dare you go off without telling us. Don't you ever do that again." But that would surely have killed the excitement in that young girl. Instead, she saw my shining eyes and sat down to hear the wonderful story of how a hen lays an egg.

The reason I like this story is that it illustrates that I had the making of a little scientist: curiosity, asking questions, not getting the right answer, deciding to find out for myself, making a mistake, not giving up, learning patience. A different mother might have crushed that early curiosity, and I might not be sitting here with you today.

It was indeed wonderful that my childhood love of animals along with the support of my mother led to my saving up money to get to Africa, and meeting the late Louis Leakey, who offered me this extraordinary opportunity to go and study not just any animal—I would have been prepared to study anything to be out in the bush—but chimpanzees, our closest living relatives. We share 98.7% of our DNA with them.

JC: A little scientist was born. I would claim that's how theologians are also born. You talked about being in stillness and in silence, waiting patiently rather than trying to rush things by taking the initiative yourself and perhaps overpowering the situation. Maybe there's something deeply spiritual in that experience itself.

JG: I should come back to David Greybeard; because I went off track. After four months, David Greybeard was the first chimpanzee to begin to lose his fear of me. He was extremely handsome and exceptionally gentle. He was not the top-ranking male, but he was definitely a leader. He was always reassuring the subordinates, and they would follow him. On a never-to-be-forgotten day, I saw him sitting on

Jane Goodall with Mr. H. at Halki Summit I (2012)

a termite mound: breaking off stems of grass, pushing them in, and eating the termites off the stem. He was even breaking off leafy twigs to use as tools; he had to strip the leaves and the side branches. David Greybeard was using and making tools! At that time, Western scientists in their great arrogance thought that humans—and only humans—made and used tools. In fact, we were labeled "Man: The Tool-Maker." When I sent Louis Leakey this information, he was so excited. He said, "Well, now we must redefine man, redefine tool, or accept chimpanzees as humans." That enabled him to approach the *National Geographic Society*, and they offered to fund my research once the original six-months' grant ran out.

Eventually, after about seven months, David Greybeard let me follow him. One day, as I was following him through a tangle of vegetation, I got caught up with my hair and my clothes. As a result, I lost him. I thought to myself: "Well, I'll find him another day." But once I freed myself from that entanglement, I noticed that he was sitting right there, looking back as though he had been waiting for me. Maybe he was, I don't know. So I sat down near him. Lying on the ground between us was a ripe, red oil palm nut. Chimps love these. I picked it up and held it out towards him on my hand. He turned his head away, so I put my hand closer. He turned and looked directly into my eyes. He reached out, took, and dropped the nut and then with one movement, very gently squeezed my fingers, which is how chimpanzees reassure each other. In that moment, I believe that we communicated with the kind of communication that must have preceded human language. And I think it was that moment that made me realize I would be spending the rest of my life doing whatever I could to find out more about chimpanzees and to conserve them and their habitat.

JC: What is it about chimpanzees that appealed to you, that attracted you?

JG: Well, let me say first of all that I did not choose chimpanzees—that was Leakey. But once I started to study them, I became increasingly fascinated. As I look back over the sixty-five years of that study, the thing that stands out so vividly is how like us they actually are. For example, when they greet one another, they may kiss, embrace, hold hands, or pat one another on the back. When they want to show their dominance, they swagger and bristle and may shake their fists. When they want to share the food of another, they often beg by holding out their hand, palm up. Their emotions—such as happiness, sadness, anger, frustration and so on—are so similar to ours. Like us they have a dark side and are capable of aggression and even a kind of primitive warfare. But they can also show true altruism as when an unrelated individual adopts an infant whose mother has died, and they may save his or her life.

Chimps have a really complex social community. There are tremendous differences in personality, and this also extends to differences in maternal behavior. We know that what is so interesting to the human child psychologists and psychiatrists is the tremendous importance of early experience. Among chimpanzees, as in humans, we find that the kind of mothering you have as an infant will help determine who you become as you grow older and move out into society. And most important is to have a supportive mother.

Today we are still learning about those amazing chimpanzees, collecting life histories, asking questions as to whether certain behaviors are learned or innate. And by the way, most

Jane Goodall with His All-Holiness Ecumenical Patriarch Bartholomew at Halki Summit I (2012)

don't live longer than forty-five to fifty years in the wild, though they can live for over seventy in captivity when they have a plentiful supply of good food and can be treated when they are sick.

JC: Tell us something more about how you communicated with David Greybeard after that. Did you learn to speak his language?

JG: Well, we don't actually try to communicate with the wild chimps. But you want me to demonstrate how the chimpanzees greet each other, don't you?

JC: I didn't explicitly say so, but yes.

JG: I'm greeting all of you now . . . [chimpanzee pant hoot] . . . that means "Me, Jane." Each chimpanzee has his or her individual 'pant hoot.' They typically travel in small groups with individuals joining or leaving throughout the day. Sometimes they travel alone, and mothers may travel with their offspring, infants and juveniles, often adolescents, and sometimes adults, especially adult daughters. They gather in larger groups when a new food source becomes available. This is known as a fusion/fission society and the pant hoot enables scattered individuals to remain in contact with each other.

After I had been in Gombe about a year I got a letter from Leakey saying that he wanted the scientific community to take me seriously, and I had to have a degree. He had got me into Cambridge University to work for a PhD in animal behavior. As you can imagine, I was nervous. Can you imagine what I felt when I was told that I had done everything wrong? "Jane, you shouldn't have given the chimpanzees names. The correct method in science is to number your subjects." Well, the truth is I didn't think of them as subjects; I felt that I was *learning from them*. And I was told: "You can't talk about chimpanzees having personalities or minds or emotions." Why? "Because those qualities are unique to humans." Fortunately, I had a wonderful teacher when I was young who taught me that the professors were quite wrong, and that was my dog, Rusty.

Eventually, because the chimpanzees are so like us not only behaviorally, but also biologically—we share 98.7% of our DNA with them—Western science was forced to admit that we humans are not, after all, separated from the rest of the animal kingdom, and are not the only sentient, sapient beings of the planet. And it was truly helpful when the *National Geographic* magazine sent filmmaker Hugo van Lawick to Gombe to capture the fascinating behavior of the chimpanzees. This not only validated my descriptions of their behavior but captivated the hearts of people—including scientists—first in America and Europe and then in many countries around the world. I never confronted science about it. I just went on talking about how chimpanzees are, and then the film came to substantiate this. That has opened the door for us to understand that we humans are not the only beings on the planet with personalities, minds, and emotions. And this opened the door for science to look at other animals in a different light. Today people understand that not only do we find intelligence and emotions in apes and monkeys, but also in whales and dolphins, as well as elephants and in all mammals and birds studied. We have even learned how incredibly intelligent rats are. If you don't believe me, look up the video "Five Smart Rats" on Google. You'll be amazed. And giant forest rats have been trained, using their incredible sense of smell, to detect land mines left in the ground after a long civil war. I have watched

Jane Goodall at the Huffington Ecumenical Institute at HCHC (2023)

them being trained at the APOPO Centre in Tanzania. They have helped to clear all landmines in Mozambique and are now working in Angola and Cambodia. Not only clever, but charming!

Some of you have surely seen *My Octopus Teacher*. It seems that the octopus—so unlike us—is incredibly intelligent. And pigs are as intelligent as dogs, sometimes even more so. Have you heard about the South African artist called not Picasso but Pi*g*casso. This particular pig was rescued on her way to slaughter, on her way to ending up as bacon, by a local artist, who runs a small sanctuary for rescued farm animals. One day, she noticed that this pig was watching her when she painted. So she set up an easel and put a paintbrush in the pig's mouth. And at once she made a painting. Look up "Pigcasso" on the internet and you will be enchanted to see her joy when she is offered a paintbrush, the joy she shows as she creates her paintings. Her finished works sell for $5,000 and more, and helps to finance the sanctuary. She has already had two exhibitions!

JC: Why did you leave Gombe? Why did you decide to abandon your beautiful life and friends there?

JG: Many people wonder why I did not stay with the chimps. It was indeed a wonderful time in my life, when I could spend hours learning about the forest ecosystem, out in nature with the chimpanzees, or alone. I built up a small research station and loved spending time with the students and the Tanzanian field staff as we shared our observations. The change came in 1986. By this time, I had just obtained my PhD and was writing scientific papers as well as articles for the general public. But then in 1986 I helped to arrange a conference in Chicago; and, for the first time, we brought together the seven other field groups also studying chimpanzees in Africa and some scientists doing non-invasive research on chimpanzees in captivity. At this conference we had a session on conservation, and I think we were all shocked because it became clear that forests were being destroyed across their range and chimpanzee numbers had plummeted from something probably close to two million, a hundred years ago, to about three hundred thousand maximum, spread over twenty-one nations. This was a result of habitat destruction, the growth of the bush meat trade (the commercial hunting of wild animals for sale), shooting moth-

Jane Goodall with His All-Holiness Ecumenical Patriarch Bartholomew at Halki Summit I (2012)

ers to steal their infants for sale as pets or for entertainment and, in those days, for medical research. Also there was human population growth, and people were moving into the forest habitat of the chimpanzees. At that conference there was a session on conditions in captivity, and we saw secretly filmed footage from a medical research lab showing these closest relatives of ours, who are so like us in so many ways, confined alone—and they are such social beings—in five-foot-by-five-foot cages; some of them had been there for twenty years or more. Their only interactions with people were when lab assistants in white coats came and stuck needles into them. In many ways this resembles solitary confinement for prisoners, many of whom, like the chimps, have been guilty of no crime. The chimps were imprisoned because they are biologically so like us that they can be infected with our infectious diseases and, so it was thought, they could help scientists find cures and vaccines for various diseases. Almost all that research was not useful.

So, when I left that conference, I didn't make any conscious decision to stop doing my scientific work at Gombe; it just happened. I went as a scientist and left as an activist. I call it my Damascus moment as it reminds me of the change in St. Paul on his journey to Damascus. And since that day I have very seldom been more than three weeks consecutively in one place.

JC: So you left Gombe, but you really didn't. You remained passionate about conserving the environment that you researched and fell in love with. Where did you go, and what did you do?

JG: I started off traveling through Africa to some of the chimpanzee range countries in order to learn more about the problems they faced. But at the same time, I learned a great deal about the plight of many Africans living in and around chimpanzee habitat: the crippling poverty, the lack of health and education facilities, and the degradation of their farmland as their populations grew. It all came to a head when I flew over the tiny Gombe National Park and the surrounding area. When I began my study in 1960, Gombe was part of the great forest equatorial belt that stretched to the West Coast. Looking down from the plane, I was absolutely shocked to see the extent of the deforestation outside the park. The only trees left were in the really steep valleys where even desperate farmers couldn't cultivate. It was also clear that there were more people living there than the land could support. So, in their struggle to survive, they were cutting down trees for charcoal or timber in order to make money or to make more land to grow more food. And it hit me then: if we don't help these people to find a way of making a living *without* destroying their environment, we can't save chimps, forests, or anything else.

So, we at the Jane Goodall Institute [JGI] began our community-led conservation program, Tacare "take care". It began *not* with a group of arrogant white people going into the twelve villages around Gombe, but seven carefully selected local Tanzanians who sat down with the villagers and asked them what JGI could do to help. So, we started by restoring fertility to the overused farmland *without* the terrible chemical pesticides and artificial fertilizers that are used in industrial agriculture and have a terrible effect on many species of plants and animals, kill the soil, and often make humans sick. At the same time, we worked with local Tanzanian authorities to improve health and education. And then we raised money to provide as many scholarships as we could to give young girls a chance of attending and completing secondary education that was a privilege only for boys at the time in poor communities. Then we provided microfinance programs, pioneered by Muhammad Yunus—the Bangladeshi economist, entrepreneur, and Nobel Prize laureate—so that people could start their own small, environmentally sustainable businesses. We also provided family planning information. The women at that time were giving birth to ten or more children. Family planning was well received as women were starting to understand that one of the best ways out of poverty is a good education for their children and there were few who could afford to educate large families.

We later introduced GIS and GPS technology and trained volunteers from the surrounding area to monitor the health of their village forest reserves using smart phones and iPads to record illegal activities. And satellite imagery enabled the villagers to complete their land use management plans, setting aside areas for wildlife.

This program has been very successful. It is now in 104 villages throughout most of the chimp range in Tanzania and is working in six other African countries as well. The people

Jane Goodall with His All-Holiness Ecumenical Patriarch Bartholomew at the Templeton Prize Ceremony (2025)

understand that protecting and restoring the environment is not just about protecting wildlife; it's for their own future.

JC: So, what has been the impact of colonialism on the people and their relationship to the land?

JG: The sad thing is that even today, although many Africans are much better off than they were, there is still so much poverty everywhere, and still so many children with no chance of a good education. And a lot of this is the legacy of colonialism. Unfortunately the exploitation of Africans and African resources continues today with some of the big corporations, especially mining, oil and gas and timber, moving in and doing exactly what was done in the old colonial days, leaving Africans—hundreds of thousands of Africans—poorer than they were before, often dispossessed of their land and forced to work for the companies that were responsible for their plight.

One of my saddest memories was visiting a group of Twa (once called pygmies) who had been forced from the forest that was their home when it was made into a forest reserve. They were moved to some land outside and told to farm. Not only was the land degraded, but they did not know how to farm. I have seldom seen such a dispirited group of people. And this has been happening to indigenous people in many places. I was so pleased that a group from "Roots & Shoots" [a JGI program to benefit the environment and improve the lives of people and animals] went to their rescue, teaching and helping them to farm and find ways of making a living.

JC: But you didn't stay permanently in Africa. Why did you decide to leave?

JG: It was sometime in the 1980s that I began to travel outside Africa so that I could spread awareness about the plight of people, chimps, and other wildlife. This was when I learned, firsthand, about the problems facing our planet today: pollution, climate change, loss of species, industrial farming, and the crazy idea that there can be unlimited economic development on a planet with finite resources *and* a growing population.

JC: You now travel the whole world encouraging, educating, and inspiring people, especially young children. A major focus of the "Roots &

Jane Goodall at the Huffington Ecumenical Institute at HCHC (2023)

Shoots" program is *caring*—caring about people and caring about the planet.

JG: Yes, caring about people, animals, and the environment.

JC: Which, by the way, as I was wondering last night, is what the word "conversation" implies. I was ruminating on our upcoming interview this morning and thought: "This won't be a conversation. People aren't here to listen to me; even I'm not here to listen to me. All of us want to listen to you." But I looked up the word, and "conversation" doesn't just mean "talking;" it literally means "leaning into one another" and even helping one another. That is exactly what you do. You teach people that there are connections between the work you did in the jungle, the work you do with animals, and the work you think people should be doing with one other and with the rest of creation. If we were to adopt different terminology, we might call it social justice or creation care—in other words, it is all about caring for each other.

Tell us a bit about how you share that vision with all those who attend your talks, and especially with young people.

JG: Well, I tell them about JGI's truly community-led conservation program, Tacare, that I told you about earlier. And I emphasize that we are, all of us, part of the natural world; and in fact, we depend on it for food, water, air—everything. But we depend on healthy ecosystems made up of a complex and interdependent combination of animals and plants, each one with a unique role to play. If you think of an ecosystem as a beautiful, living tapestry, then every time one of those animals or plants disappears, it's like pulling a thread from the tapestry until the entire fabric hangs in tatters and the ecosystem collapses. And that's what is happening around the world.

JC: And how did you end up involving young people?

JG: Well, it was when I began travelling around the world, to raise awareness about the grim situation in much of Africa. And even back then in the 1980s, I was meeting young people who were beginning to lose hope. I encountered this all over the world. Some of them, perhaps most of them, were just apathetic; they didn't seem to care about anything. Others were angry, even violent. A few seemed depressed, some clinically depressed.

I began talking to them in these different countries—from China to America, from Europe to Africa, from the Middle East to Australia—and they all told me more or less the same feelings: "Well, you've compromised our future and there's nothing we can do about it." And it's true; we *have* compromised the future of young people. We have actually been *stealing* their future probably from the time of the Industrial Revolution. Nevertheless, what I felt was clearly wrong was when they protested "there is nothing that we can do about it." And that is when our humanitarian and environmental program, "Roots & Shoots," began. It started with twelve high school students who came to see me in my home in Tanzania. And by the way, it's sort of interesting: twelve villages around Gombe, twelve students who started "Roots & Shoots." It's sort of coincidental, or maybe miraculous . . .?

JC: I wouldn't argue with that.

JG: Anyway, these twelve students were concerned about different things. Some worried about the illegal dynamite fishing where sticks

Sienna meets her "idol" Jane Goodall at the Huffington Ecumenical Institute at HCHC (2023)

of dynamite were being stolen, thrown into the water and the stunned fish—when they floated dead to the surface—were scooped up in nets. And this was destroying the coral reefs in the region. Some were worried about poaching in their national parks; why wasn't the government doing anything about this? The government was very corrupt back then. A few of them were worried about street children with no homes or security. Others were upset about the way stray dogs were being treated. There were so many different concerns. So I asked them to gather their friends together and we had a meeting of about thirty young people. "Roots & Shoots" was born at that meeting. Its principal message, which is true for every one of us, is: "Every day that you spend on this planet, you make some kind of impact! And unless you're living in extreme poverty, or are very young, then you can choose what kind of impact you make."

And because everything is interrelated, we decided that each group would choose three projects in order to make the world a better place: one would help people raise money either for the local community or for refugees and so on; another would make things better for animals, including domestic animals; and a third would help the natural environment. Of course, a group could select a single project that would encompass all three areas. "Roots & Shoots" now operates in more than seventy-five countries around the planet, and its members range from preschool and kindergarten to university and beyond. Even senior citizens get together and form their own "Roots & Shoots" groups, and they tell me "This has changed our lives. We now have a meaning, a purpose." We've had three groups formed in prisons!

"Roots & Shoots" is flexible, so the projects chosen will vary depending on the age of the group, their environment, their socioeconomic status, their culture and their religion. We don't tell them what to do; they choose themselves. When you choose a project that you are passionate about, you will work with commitment and passion. And when you take action and make a difference, you no longer feel helpless and hopeless.

JC: And "Roots & Shoots" exists in every state here in the United States?

JG: Yes, every state. Your community here could start a group. Or a family could initiate a group. It mostly thrives in schools and universities. One group consists only of two brothers. Another is a grandmother, her four daughters, their children, and one adopted disabled child.

People often ask me, "Why did you call the program 'Roots & Shoots?'" I tell them, "Think of a big tree. It probably grew from a small seed. When it started to germinate, little roots appeared and a small shoot. You could pick it up and it would seem so small, so weak. Yet there is a magic—a life force so powerful that those little roots grow and ultimately push aside rocks in order to reach water. The little shoots can work their way through cracks in a brick wall to reach the sunlight and eventually the wall will collapse. We see the rocks and the walls as the problems of the world and the hundreds and thousands of young people—the roots and the shoots—have the power to overcome those problems."

JC: Say something more about children's relationship with animals.

JG: One of the problems today is that our children are becoming increasingly separated from nature, spending most of their time on social media. It has been scientifically proved that time in nature is important for the psychological development of very young children. And time in nature is important for adults too, for both our physical and mental health. It is also essential that children learn to be kind to animals, as it has been proved that children who are cruel to animals will often become violent adults, more likely to start a school shooting or something similar.

JC: We have talked about nature and the environment. But let's talk about the bad news. You have served as a United Nations Messenger of Peace. I want you to tell us what you think about the wars all over the world. What is their impact on the planet? I mean, we should be concerned about all wars. But one that I think has literally changed my whole mindset is the most recent one, namely Russia's invasion of Ukraine.

As I said earlier, I was just in Budapest for an environmental conference, which was ironically being held at a state university that used to be a military school. I believe the university still retains an academic department that trains the military. And there was a "major general" at the conference who was speaking on the same panel as I was; and so I couldn't resist. I wanted to ask what he felt about the impact of the military on the environment. But I don't think he understood my question. He basically told me how the Hungarian army is very careful about switching the lights off in order to save energy. He even told me—I had no idea, but it makes sense—that tanks have accelerator pedals, and they advise their soldiers not to press too hard on them. I began to think: "I wonder about an armored tank compared to my Toyota Prius!" But most of all, I was hoping that he might explain what he feels was the impact of a military assault or even or a military defense on the natural environment, on the natural resources of the planet. After all, war is often a war of and over resources. Armies seek to deplete the water, destroy the energy of the enemy. And they do that in a calculated, deliberate manner. We see this in the aggression of Russia on Ukraine. Should a nation be accountable for this kind of action? Should the military be responsible for this kind of damage? What do you say and what do you see?

JG: Well, first of all, I think he perfectly well understood your question, but he wasn't about to answer it. He simply skirted around it. If you look at the analysis of what's creating greenhouse gases, for example, they mention industrial agriculture, and they also mention the burning of fossil fuels and industrial agriculture. But they almost never mention the military. Even without actual war, there is the preparation for conflict: testing new fighter jets, submarines, even testing nuclear weapons deep in the ocean. The damage to the environment, the amount of CO_2 added to the atmosphere is staggering. Yet, as I said, it is almost never mentioned. The amount of fossil fuel that is burned during modern warfare is, of course, having a huge impact on climate change. Then think of Vietnam and the Agent Orange that was used to defoliate the trees to make it easier to kill "the enemy," the Viet Cong. And the constant bombing of cities in Ukraine resulting in the destruction of hundreds of buildings, which will all have to be replaced using precious, finite natural resources. Animals are especially vulnerable in times of war. Their habitats are being destroyed. Land mines set across large areas may remain in the ground long after a war has ended, and this has led to thousands of people losing a foot or a leg. And it can affect animals too; one elephant, for example, lost her foot. There can be no doubt that war has a major effect on the environment.

And we should not forget the devastating effect of war on human communities. Remember, I lived through World War II and saw returning service men and those injured during bombing raids—most horribly injured, many having lost a limb or suffered severe burns. And the images of the horrors endured during the Holocaust changed my mind about humanity forever. It brought me face to face with pure evil. We all said: "Never again!" Yet, it has happened.

As for being a UN Messenger of Peace, you ask me what does that mean? I think they chose me because of the "Roots & Shoots" program. We try to bring young people together from different countries, cultures, and religions in order for them to grow an appreciation and gain an understanding that what is far more important than the color of your skin, or your language, or your culture, or your religion, is the fact we are all human beings. We all can laugh. We all can cry. And we all can love.

Sadly, of course, it seems that so many of us can also hate. You know, it is becoming increasingly apparent today, from paleontological records, that Louis Leakey was right when he said there was a common ancestor about six million years ago, a chimp-like, human-like ape. Louis believed that behavior shown by chimps and humans today may have been handed down from that common ancestor, to both chimps and humans as we evolved along our separate paths. When I discovered that chimps can be violent and aggressive and even may engage in primitive war, I was shocked and saddened. It made them even more like us than I had thought. But even more shocking is the fact that we humans, despite our incredible intellect, have been unable to control those aggressive tendencies despite the six million years of evolution. You cannot look around the world and say that human beings don't have an aggressive streak, can you? Look at domestic violence. Look at conflict within families and communities. And look at conflict between cultures and ethnic groups, as well as between nations. And we not only have that aggressive streak, but we have developed something that makes us worse than chimps. Only we are capable of deliberate cruelty, of deliberate torture of other humans. In fact, we can use our intellect to devise the most horrific forms of torture.

Chimps are actually very good at resolving conflict. They're uneasy when there is conflict within the group. In chimp society, "might is right"! So, after a fight, it is the victim who will nervously approach the aggressor, often with outstretched hand, and very often the aggressor will then pat their victim on the hand or head.

The biggest difference between them and us is the explosive development of our intellect. Yet we cannot claim to be intelligent. We have all seen that photograph of our beautiful, blue-and-green planet surrounded by the cold, black immensity of the outer space. That little globe is our only home, and we are destroying it. That is why I say we are *intellectual* rather than *intelligent*. We seem to have lost the wisdom shown by so many indigenous peoples: that before making a decision, we should consider how it will affect future generations. Yet now people are mainly concerned about how my decision will affect *me, now*: "me and my family; my next shareholders meeting; my next political campaign." There seems to be a disconnect between our clever brain and our caring heart, and I truly believe that only when the head and the heart work in harmony can we attain our true human potential, which is huge.

JC: We're back to religious overtones again. You are speaking of the head and the heart. I think this is what people appreciate about you: you are the real thing, you really are. There are not too many people in the world that I can say that about. I think of Pope Francis as another example. By the way, Pope Francis is coming out with a sequel to *Laudato Si'*, entitled *Laudate Deum*.[2]

JG: I know. I've been asked to write a little piece for it.

JC: It's a big deal. He talks about war. We've been through two world wars, and the third world war is our war against nature. The new encyclical will be out in a few days, probably on St. Francis day, in early October.

JG: Do Orthodox Christians bless animals in churches?

JC: We certainly do. We also have certain specific prayers for animals from centuries ago.

JG: You do? Because twice, in Grace Cathedral in San Francisco, I was asked to give a sermon. All the animals were there to be blessed and, on one of those occasions, one of the strang-

---

[2] *Laudate Deum: To All People of Good Will on the Climate Crisis* was issued on October 4, 2023.

est things happened. There were dogs and cats and parrots and parakeets—everything down to a rat in a cage. Even two policemen on horses were standing inside the cathedral. The noise was unbelievable. I mean, you couldn't hear the poor man reading the scripture lesson. Dogs growled at each other and sometimes barked, despite the efforts of their embarrassed owners to stop them. And you know how noisy parrots and parakeets can be; those screeches! Well, when I climbed up to the pulpit to deliver my sermon, after I had been speaking for about three minutes, I suddenly stopped and said: "Listen!" There was dead silence. It reminded me of the time when St. Francis of Assisi asked the birds who were singing loudly to be quiet while he said his evening prayers. I never believed that story, but I do now. For an entire twenty minutes there was not a single sound. It actually happened, and it's recorded. Isn't that amazing?

JC: That's amazing indeed. We do have prayers. I think it's unfortunate that in our churches, we have retained these prayers as a remnant from a medieval past. We are proud of and romanticize these prayers, but we don't actually hold many services for domestic or wild tropical animals—at least, not as much as you'll find in other churches today. In fact, that's a larger problem in our church. I think that Orthodox sometimes find it difficult to connect their traditional past to the present situation. Perhaps the most exotic thing we have in our church today are the vestments worn by clergy.

But you spoke about the head and the heart. You also spoke about doing something good, of making an impact, of doing at least one thing of lasting importance every day. These are also inherently spiritual matters; at least, this is the way I feel about them. You don't just talk the talk, but you walk the talk. That is surely what we are supposed to be preaching to people from the pulpit. How would you advise people to do that? How can you convince them that small, even insignificant daily actions can permanently improve the condition of people, the protection of animals, and the sustainability of the environment?

JG: You know, so many people come to me who have lost hope. They say: "Well, there's nothing I can do. I'm just one person. What I do won't change anything in the long run." Indeed, if you look around the world today, I defy any thinking, caring person not to feel depressed.

It is disheartening. And it is not only the environment that is at risk; it's the wider social and especially political state today. It is the fact that religions fight against each other and fight among themselves—literally disobeying every single rule and breaking every single commandment that is held precious in their sacred books. Look, for instance, at the Jews and the Palestinians.

I say to people who feel depressed: "You cannot save the world. But you can go back to your community, gather some friends together, and figure out what you care about. You might care about single-use plastic that is destroying wildlife, especially in the ocean. Or you might care about poverty. You might care about the people who are hungry. You might care about the homeless. Whatever it is that you feel passionate about, get together with others, talk about it, and do something." Then you feel will better. And when you begin to feel better, you will want to do even more. And others will be inspired to help. It is *action* that brings hope to the hopeless. And without hope we fall into apathy and do nothing.

So I say to people: "If you do one thing, and it is just you, it won't make any difference. But it's not just you. All around the world there are people who care. If you put together millions and perhaps billions of small ethical choices each day, you are making a huge difference."

I always suggest that people think about the products they are buying. When they were made, did it harm the environment? Was it cruel to animals? Is it cheap because of unfair wages? Then don't buy it. Will an ethically produced product be more expensive? Probably, but then we will value it more and waste less, and human waste is a huge problem today. We can choose what to buy. We can choose to move to a plant-based diet. Meat eating, especially heavy meat eating, is having a devastating effect on the environment. Huge areas of land are cleared to grow food to feed the animals incarcerated in factory farms; more corn is grown to feed these prisoners than to feed starving people. It takes a lot of water to change vegetable to animal protein. And in their digestion they all produce methane, a virulent greenhouse gas. And this is all in addition to the horrendous cruelty to the animals themselves, especially when we now know that they are *all* sentient beings, individuals with personalities, able to feel fear, frustration, and, of course, pain. Many are very intelligent, especially pigs.

JC: Jane, I don't want to take much more of your time. You've already made a huge impact on all of us today, I can assure you of that. What you've achieved here—as I told you would happen when I invited you, even before you came—will leave an impression and will cause ripple effects. I am profoundly grateful to you for taking time to meet with us, literally on your way by car from Plymouth to New York City. I've seen the way you sit and work in the back seat of a car crammed with luggage and books. You're tireless, and I'm truly grateful for adding us to your busy schedule. What else would you like to say?

JG: Well, I would like you to hear my reasons for staying hopeful. I'm asked all the time: "Jane, you can't possibly have hope? You know so much about what's going on in the world. You've seen forests disappear. You've seen chimp numbers drop. You've seen the violence in the world. You've seen the results of war on the environment, on people, and on animals. And you've seen or heard about horrible acts of cruelty."

Well, my first reason for hope are the young people. Everywhere I go, I find that once they understand the problems and are empowered to take action, nothing can stop them. I've just travelled from Tanzania and Uganda to Japan and South Korea, and everywhere young people are the same. At the end of our "Roots & Shoots" gatherings, we say together: "We can!" We *can* slow down climate change. We *can* slow down loss of biodiversity. We know what we have to do. But do we have the will to do it? Do we have the will to tighten our belts one notch because something made ethically costs a few pennies more? The children are the ones who are standing up and saying together: "Together, we *can* and together we *will*!" And I say: "Yes, because together we *must* change the world!"

That is arguably my greatest reason for hope. Do you believe that if you aim for the stars, you might reach the moon? If you aim only for the moon, you might reach the top of Everest. So I aim for the stars. I want "Roots & Shoots" in every school. I know that won't happen, but it is spreading so rapidly because people want hope; children need hope and parents need hope. If you bring a little child into the world, you must give that child hope.

My second reason for hope is our intellect. Unfortunately, however, we so often do not use our intellect wisely. We have designed technology to destroy, the technology of war, of mining, of industrial farming. But scientists are beginning to work hard to create technology that will enable us to live in greater harmony, less destructively with the natural world. And as individuals, more and more people are beginning to think of their own environmental footprints each day.

My third reason for hope is that nature is resilient. I talked earlier about the bare hills around Gombe. There are no bare hills anymore; the trees have gradually come back as seeds that had lain dormant in the ground sometimes for years, germinated when the farmers stopped working on the steep hills. We did some tree planting, but mostly it was natural regeneration.

I cannot resist telling a little story here. Some date palm seeds from the long-ago palm groves of Lebanon were discovered in the ruins of an ancient army garrison. Obviously, some soldiers had been eating dates and throwing the seeds on the floor. That was two-thousand years ago! An Israeli botanist was entrusted with three of the precious seeds, and managed to get one of them to germinate. The resulting palm was a male and named "Methuselah." Because she had been so successful, she was given a few more of those precious seeds, and so "Hannah" emerged. Now "Hannah" has been pollinated by "Methuselah," and I was actually sent three of the very first dates produced from this union! I don't actually like dates, but those three—grown from seeds that had lain on the stone floor for 2000 years—were quite different, and delicious!!! That story perfectly illustrates the resilience of nature. And I have seen or heard about so many places where nature has returned in regions we have previously destroyed. Like the trees that have returned to the hills around Gombe, animals on the brink of extinction have been given a second chance because there are people who refuse to sit by and allow them to vanish.

Finally, there is another reason for hope: namely, the indomitable human spirit. People who tackle what seems to be impossible and refuse to give up. Think of Nelson Mandela and Martin Luther King, Jr. But we also have modern examples. I have just been with a young Kenyan man, who was sent for studies at university in Alaska and was lost for three days in a snowdrift. He managed to escape and find his way to a hospital. When he woke up, his feet had been amputated due to frostbite. Amazingly, however, his hands still functioned. Now, he travels everywhere and has even won a couple of New York marathons by using running blades as prosthetics on his lower limbs. I invited him up to the stage in Plymouth where he now lives, and there he was on his blades, showing the audience how he can jump up and down. There was a fireman in the audience; I called him, too, up to the stage. He had lost one leg, but he is back on the force, the only fireman with a prosthetic.

The indomitable human spirit is manifest everywhere around us. That's why I carry Mr. H. [an adorable, small stuffed monkey] with me wherever I go. Can you see Mr. H in the back? I will hold him up for you. Mr. H was given to me about thirty years ago by Gary Haun, a man who thought he was giving me a stuffed chimpanzee for my birthday. I made him hold the tail and told him chimps don't have tails. He said: "Never mind. Take him with you wherever you go and you'll know that my spirit is with you."[3]

Gary lost his eyesight in the United States Marines at the age of just twenty-one. As he was learning to live in this new, dark world, for some bizarre reason he decided that he wanted to become a magician. Everybody told him: "How can you be a magician if you're blind?" Yet he now performs shows for children. He lays out his props beforehand. And the children don't even know that he is blind. At the end, he tells them and says: "Something might go wrong in your life, because we never know. But if it does, don't ever give up. There is always a way forward." Today, he does sky-diving and cross-country skiing. He has also taught himself to paint. If any of you are interested in seeing a portrait of Mr. H, whom Mr. Haun has never seen but only felt, there is a little book you can purchase on Amazon called, *Blind Artist*, by Gary Haun.

---

[3] Mr. H and Jane go back thirty years. Inspired by Gary's perseverance, Jane turned her birthday present into a motivational mascot for the Jane Goodall Institute. Held by thousands—if not millions—of people across almost one hundred countries, Jane says that the hope and inspiration that Mr. H represents rubs off on everyone who touches him.

At any rate, I need to end. Perhaps I should have stopped sooner but I wanted to give my reasons for hope. You know, we all need hope. Here is another reason for hope [as Jane addresses a young disabled girl in her audience]: You're going to do "Roots & Shoots," aren't you?

JC: She actually loves animals; she has loved them ever since kindergarten and wants to become a zookeeper.

JG: Oh, good. A zookeeper, that's what you want to be? Well, go to one of the good zoos because there are still a lot of bad zoos.
(*Young girl:* I'll try my best!)

JG: Well, that is exactly what my mother used to say to me: "If you do your best, that's perfect." Whereas my father used to say: "You got a B at school? Why didn't you get an A?"

JC: That sounds like a lot of fathers I know . . .
Jane, perhaps you can offer a final word for the community here on this campus, where most of these students, men and women, are training to take up leadership positions in church communities. Along with starting a "Roots & Shoots" program, what would you advise them?

JG: Well, I would say we need the different faith communities and all religious believers to come together and understand that protecting the environment is the most important issue of all. Without a safe network of ecosystems, we are doomed. We all need to get together and take action—whoever we are, no matter how old or young we are, whatever faith we profess. Even if we have no faith, we need to work together to heal the planet for the sake of all life on Planet Earth.

We have got to address the human problems and show how all of these things are interconnected and how contact between the natural world and that of the spirit—of morality and ethics—is ever so precious and all too important.

JC: How do we do something about this? How exactly do we spread that message to the general public? What are the barriers in this effort to restore interconnectedness in a stifling urban setting?

JG: In many ways, it's almost like the death of spirit that I'm finding as I go around the world. This materialistic lifestyle of ours makes life meaningless. It's been shown, scientifically, that children growing up surrounded by nature develop in a psychologically healthier way. You can re-green a part of the inner city, which was high in crime rate, and that crime rate will drop. You need a connection with nature and yet what are we doing to our children today? There are children surrounded by concrete and some who have never even seen a tree. What is that doing to their psyche? And how can they feel connected to a great spiritual power when it's just concrete that they see around them? Yes, there are beautiful buildings, but we make less and less of those. We're making cement squares, ugly cement blocks. It's a very sad world, this materialistic world, this Western rat race. It is not surprising really that there is conflict around the world. At least, I don't find myself surprised because the infrastructure is falling to pieces. So many people are living in a materialistic world, wanting far more than they need, while others are living in abject poverty. And we are increasingly detached from the natural world and living in virtual reality.

JC: That is true. I like to say that it's not enough to pray for a place for your soul in heaven if your children don't have a place for their body on earth.

Jane, you have given us compelling motives to want to be on earth. You have given us several reasons to hope. And you have left your indelible mark here on this campus, on this community, and on this city. We are all so very grateful to you.

www.ingramcontent.com/pod-product-compliance
Lightning Source LLC
LaVergne TN
LVHW011048110826
845149LV00015B/3406

9781960613134